Sneaky the Hairy Mountain Monster

How I Lost My Parents

Norma Fleagane

ISBN 979-8-88943-184-8 (paperback)
ISBN 979-8-88540-242-2 (hardcover)
ISBN 979-8-88540-241-5 (digital)

Christian Faith Publishing
832 Park Avenue
Meadville, PA 16335
www.christianfaithpublishing.com

Printed in the United States of America

Makayla and Blake were visiting their grandparents for spring break. Although Makayla and Blake were a whole generation apart, they were only a year apart in age. They were sitting at the kitchen table clipping their school pictures, which were on two big photo sheets of paper. Blake was writing "Your friend, Blake" on the back of each picture. Makayla wrote "Love, Makayla" on the front bottom corner of her pictures.

Blake's mom and Aunt Tiffani were in the kitchen, baking bread and cookies for Easter. Blake and Makayla helped color and decorate Easter eggs that morning. Now that they were done clipping their pictures, they went outside to help Makayla's mom and Grandma decorate a barren tree in front of the house with colorful plastic

Easter eggs. Since Blake was taller than Makayla, he decorated the top of the tree. Makayla did the bottom.

Makayla stood back, looked at the tree, added another plastic egg or two, and with satisfaction said, "There! That's better. That looks pretty."

They went back into the house; cleaned up their scrap of papers on the table; gave their aunts, cousins, and grandma a picture; and put the rest in their pockets.

They went looking for Grandfather to give him pictures. He was sitting in his favorite chair watching the news on television.

"Oh, thank you," Grandfather said as he put the pictures in his wallet. "I'm going to show all my friends how pretty my great-granddaughter is and how handsome and big my grandson is getting."

That made Blake and Makayla smile. They put the rest of the pictures back in their pockets, gave Grandpa a hug, and told him they were going outside to play.

"What do you want to play, Makayla?" Blake picked up a football.
"You want to play football?"
    "No," Makayla said.

"How about baseball?" He pounded his fist in his baseball glove to shape it.

"No." Then she saw a soccer ball and picked it up. "Let's go kick the soccer ball around."

Blake would much rather play football or baseball, but he reluctantly said, "Oh, okay."

The sun was warm, but the air was cool, especially in the shade. They went up the street and played in an open field. They were laughing and playing while kicking the ball around.

Then Blake kicked the ball, and it started to roll down the hill. Blake and Makayla ran after it, but it kept on rolling. They finally caught up to the ball, and they both sat down on the ground, laughing.

Makayla looked around and said, "Hey, doesn't Sneaky live down there somewhere?"
Blake said, "Yes."

Makayla stood up and said excitedly, "Let's go see if he is there!"

"What? You want to go see Sneaky?" Blake said with a quizzical look on his face. "You used to be afraid of him."

"I know. I know. I was little then. I am older now. I'm ten. I am not afraid."

Blake put the soccer ball down next to a log, and they got up and ran down the hill and through brush and fallen-down tree branches and made their way to the cave where Sneaky lived.

Blake and Makayla walked up to the cave. Sneaky was there. He remembered Blake. He wasn't afraid.

He motioned to them to come in. "Sit down," Sneaky said. There were two tree logs, bark and all, on each side of a broken round wooden table, which was held up by four short tree stumps. Blake sat on one side and Makayla sat on the other side.

Sneaky was very hospitable. He offered them dandelion tea sweetened with honey he got from a tree. He put apples, nuts, and berries on plates in front of them. The dishes were not the best-looking dishes, and they did not match—they were chipped and broken. Sneaky would find things that people threw away and use them.

"I never had dandelion tea before," Blake said.

"Do you live here all by yourself?" Makayla asked.

"Yes."

"Where are your parents? Don't you have any brothers or sisters?

"I don't have any brothers or sisters, and I lost my parents in a flood."

"In a flood? What flood? What happened?" Blake questioned.

"Many years ago when I was little, it had rained for many days, and the snow from the winter started to melt as the weather warmed up. Rainwater was pouring off the hills. The creeks and river were overflowing. My parents and I were looking for food along the riverbank when we got swept away in the rushing water. We floated down the Ohio River.

I hit a downed tree in the water and grabbed hold of the tree branch. I pulled myself across the branch until I got to the riverbank. I was tired from fighting the rushing water and trying to get to safety. I lay on the riverbank and fell asleep.

"Oh my gosh! And your parents? Do you know where they are? Are they living?" Makayla asked.

"I don't know. I like to think they are. My parents were tough—and strong—and good swimmers. So I like to think they are living and we will be together again someday."

"How did you find this cave?" Blake asked.

Sneaky poured more tea as he continued to tell the story.

"One morning I woke up to find myself surrounded by a rabbit, a squirrel, a chipmunk, and two deer looking at me.

They all spoke in unison, 'Who are you? Why are you here?'

I wasn't afraid. I replied, 'I lost my parents in the flood, and I don't have any place to go. I don't have a home, and I don't know where I am.'

The rabbit, squirrel, chipmunk, and deer started whispering to each other and then started prancing around and then whispering again. 'We can't find your parents, but we know a place you can call home. Follow us.'

They led me up the hill away from the Ohio River and then down another hill to a cave nestled deep in the woods. It was obscured, surrounded by trees and shrubs. The narrow opening had vines and moss growing on the outside of the cave.

'It's not a beauty,' said the deer, 'but at least you can get out of the rain and cold.'

I went inside. The cave was nice and dry. And that is how I got this place I call home," Sneaky recounted.

"I was so excited I was no longer homeless. I thanked all the animals who found this place for me. They pranced around very pleased with themselves and then went about their business. The rabbit went back to his rabbit hole, the squirrel gathered up some more acorns and scampered up a tree to his house. The chipmunk went in a hollowed-out log, and the deer pranced up the hill and disappeared into the woods."

"I'm afraid of humans, and humans are afraid of me. When I get frightened, I roar, and fire comes out of my mouth and eyes. It just happens when I am startled and scared."

"Oh, I get it! It is a defense mechanism, like the skunk that lifts his tail and gives off a terrible odor to ward off predators when he is scared," said Blake.

"I like the birds and animals, and I like people, but I am shy. I hide. I don't want people to see me. I am self-conscious because I have three eyes. When I look around, all the animals and all the humans have two eyes. My parents had two eyes, but I have three. Do you know of any animals or humans who have three eyes?" Sneaky asked.

Makayla and Blake got to thinking real hard. "Hmmm, I can't think of any," said Makayla.

"Besides, the elephant has two eyes, but he has a trunk. Maybe he thinks he is odd because he has a trunk. The monkey has a tail and swings from trees. The kangaroo has four legs but walks on two and carries her babies in a pouch. They might think they are odd. The male deer have antlers, but the female deer do not. Some humans are tall, and some are short. Some have long hair, and some are bald. We should be happy just the way we are," Makayla said.

"Really?" Sneaky said.

"Yes, actually way, way back in time, it is believed that even humans possessed a third eye," Blake said. "In fact," Blake went on, "humans have a trace of a third eye, but it is still there buried deep inside the brain."

"So the third eye is important," Sneaky said. "When I get scared, my senses tell me there is danger, and that's when I shoot fire out of my eyes and mouth. I feel better now. I don't feel so odd."

Blake said, "Oh, there is one more thing I remember my teacher telling us. She said that there are always some species that slip through the cracks of time and possess traits that are usually long gone in their ancestors. This is probably what happened with you. You slipped through the cracks and possess the trait of three eyes like your ancestors from way, way back."

"That is very interesting. Thank you for telling me that," Sneaky said.

"You're welcome," Blake said with pride.

At that Makayla said, "We should be leaving as it will be getting dark soon."

"Thank you for inviting us in and for telling us what happened to your parents. Maybe you will find them one day," Blake said.

Makayla said, "Thank you for the tea and snacks."

As they were leaving the cave, Blake turned around and said "Sneaky, here" and handed him one of his school pictures, which was signed "Your friend, Blake."

"Oh, here's one of me too," Makayla said as she handed Sneaky one of her pictures. She gave Sneaky a quick hug and left.

As Blake and Makayla ascended the hill, they turned, and waved
to Sneaky.
Sneaky, holding Blake's hat in his hand, yelled, "You forgot your hat!"
"That's okay. You can keep it," Blake said.

Sneaky waved back, and when he couldn't see them anymore, he went into the cave. He looked at Blake's picture and read the back. He held it to his heart and said, **"I HAVE A FRIEND!"** Then he looked at Makayla's picture, which said, "Love, Makayla." Sneaky said, **"AND I AM LOVED!"**

Sneaky held the pictures close to his heart, and tears welled up in his eyes, the two on the sides, not the one on top.

Why do you think Sneaky cried?

About the Author

Norma Teichman Fleagane is a wife and mother of six daughters. She has seven grandchildren and one great-granddaughter. She was born in Ohio and studied early childhood education at Ohio University. She is a businesswoman and lives and works with her husband James in Wheeling, West Virginia, and Singer Island, Florida.